Songs of Mirabai

Songs of Mirabai

Translated by Andrew Schelling

Foreword by Arundhathi Subramaniam

WHITE PINE PRESS / BUFFALO, NEW YORK

White Pine Press
P.O. Box 236.   Buffalo, NY 14201
www.whitepine.org

Publication of this book was supported by public funds from the
New York State Council on the Arts, with the support of Governor
Kathy Hochul and the New York State Legislature, a State Agency.

Acknowledgements: Some of these translations first appeared in
Dark Ages Clasp the Daisy Root, Darshan, Notus, Parabola, and *Shambhala
Sun*. Shambhala Publications brought out the original edition in
1993. Hohm Press released a new edition in 1998. In the nearly
thirty years since their first publication, numerous journals, an-
thologies, librettos, novels, and other books have reprinted lyrics,
in North America and in India where the songs originated. Some
of these versions have been sung in America and in Wales, possibly
in other countries too. Thanks to the editors, writers, readers,
singers, and friends who pass these translations along.

Cover Image: Mayumi Oda, *Aphrodite*. Copyright © 2024 by May-
umi Oda. Used by permission of the artist.

Printed and bound in the United States of America.

ISBN 978-1-945680-78-6

Library of Congress Control Number: 2024930192

This book is dedicated to

Bertha Tigay Saposs
Corinne Schelling
Althea Rose Abruscato
Luna Luz

And to the singers, most of them women, who risk themselves on each note and have kept the lyrics alive for 500 years.

Contents

Mira shattered the manacles
of civility, family, and shame.
A latter day *gopi*, she made love explicit
for the dark Kali Yuga.
Independent, unutterably fearless,
she sang her delight for an
amorous god.
Scoundrels considered her treacherous
and ventured to kill her,
but draining like nectar the poison they sent
she came forth unscathed.
Striking the drumskin of worship
Mira cringed before no one.
Family, civility, gossip—
she shattered the manacles.
She sang praise to her lord who lifts
mountains.

—Nabhadas
from the *Bhaktamala* (ca. 1600)

Foreword

Politics in India is ablaze with the word *bhakt*. It is intended as a term of scorn, a contemptuous dismissal of those who kowtow to the politics of the far right. A *bhakt* is seen as a mindless follower, an imitator, a star-struck fan. And *bhakti*, the abstract noun from which the word is derived, is seen as uncritical obedience, slavish surrender, vanilla love. In short, spinelessness.

The current usage is deeply ironic, because nothing could be further from the truth. *Bhakti*, or sacred devotion, is, in actual fact, a complex business—molten, seething with paradox. It always has been. The deity in sacred Indian poetry can be unpunctual and whimsical, but is never a despot. The devotee may swear undying allegiance to the divine, but is no mute serf. The devotee's love of her god may be desperate, but it is never passive worship. The relationship between the human and the divine, in fact, is crazily fluid and mercurial—and for all its fluctuating power politics, implicitly mutual.

Perhaps no poet compels us to confront the swirling paradoxes of *bhakti* as much as India's best-known female mystic, Mira. Over five centuries, she has morphed from local saint of Rajasthan to world poet, her songs pervading hallowed music halls and international seminar rooms. The wild woman of Chittor, would, one suspects, be somewhat startled at the way her one-time notoriety, which seems to have turned to local sainthood in her lifetime, has now given way to posthumous global stardom.

And yet, Mira remains elusive. Domesticated by religious narratives, she has become the cliché of calendar art, where she is often presented in white, eyes closed in a state of demure sanctimony. She has also been flattened by a modern-day secular establishment into a sexy icon of female rebellion. Neither state of affairs is particularly surprising. Her rejection of social norms can still disconcert religious conservatives, and her fevered proclamations of surrender to a personal god can still be unsettling for modern readers. She stands testimony to the many ways in which the idea of *bhakti* can be defanged, distorted, trivialized.

Who *was* Mira, anyway?

Like so many figures in the Indian subcontinent's past, she stands in that blurry place between history and hagiography, part real, part cloud. Not much is known about her. Plenty is presumed. We know that she lived in the sixteenth century. That she was born to privilege. That she married a man, but yearned for another—that slippery blue god, Krishna, who consumed her, drove her to delirium, provoked her to compose poem after lyric poem in despair and rapture.

As part of the oral tradition, she has moved from individual to collective voice. Countless poems bear her imprimatur. Wherever the love of Krishna is invoked, the name of Mira cannot be far behind. Folklore, sacred literature and feminist discourse have given us a spectrum of perspectives. She has been variously viewed as docile handmaiden, bloodless saint, bold iconoclast and madwoman—the kind every woman keeps concealed in her attic. The diverse interpretations are a tribute to her haunting verse, damp with sensual abandon, that have echoed down the centuries.

And yet, the need of both scholar and devotee to join the dots can often produce a cartoon Mira, overlooking her many textures and undertones. Her love can seem, at first glance, simple. She pines. She yearns. She swoons. She does everything that lovelorn medieval women are meant to do. But on closer reading, the surprises emerge. The ethereal sprite of popular perception is also the woman willing to let down her hair, tear off her veils, wear the ankle bells of common dancing girls, peel off every last vestige of social hypocrisy and cultural restraint to get closer to her beloved god.

While she has been widely translated over the

decades, what makes these renditions by Andrew Schelling so alive and distinct is the fact that they offer us not the stylized saint, but the wild, cindering Mira. The Mira who will not be tamed by footnotes. The Mira who will not be silenced by legions of tepid imitators. The Mira who will not be prettified into pious posterhood.

This is an emotionally naked Mira, not a distant, ornamental one. A woman bewildered by *bhakti*, not exalted by it. A woman undone by love, not an entitled princess-turned-god's-pet looking beatifically heavenward. An adventurous seeker, not a sentimental songster. A woman who stumbles along a dangerous "incomprehensible road," not the obedient follower of a mainstream path. A woman in whose world "infidelity spits / like a snake" and love is "a torn heart," not a saint in pristine robes singing of an other-worldly, antiseptic love. A hoarse Mira, not a dulcet one. A disquieting Mira, not a docile one. A woman of nerve, not sentiment. Of provocation and desolation, not simpering platitudes.

This Mira waits, but she also acts. She is a pioneer in her own right, walking the "razor thin path" of those bitten by the snake venom of sacred love. She is capable of despondence, but she is also aware that seemingly arid phases can be alchemical, transforming pain into a "delicious" blessing. She is lyrical, but she is also urgent and ravenous. Hers is not a covert love. She is ready to shriek it from the rooftops. She will not settle for respectability and subterfuge. She is quite clear: she wants her god and she wants him now. There is nothing bland or pastel about this woman's life choices. She will settle for nothing less than a life dyed an iridescent, intoxicating blue.

These translations reveal a woman capable of surrender. But this surrender is never the absence of spine. Mira is capable of sounding breathless. But this breathlessness is never mere self-abasement. Even when she proclaims that she is a *dasi*, a servant, she never loses her essential spirit. This Mira reminds us that *bhakti* is not submission, but alert receptivity. That true devotion is a deep yowl of the heart, not creamy greeting-card verse. That sacred love is tough, ferocious and self-annihilating, not an erotic adolescent fantasy.

I find myself turning to these sinewy translations today to be reminded of Mira's immediacy, her *nowness*. And to be reminded that she belongs to many. She belongs to the haunting voices of the folk singers of western India, their voices fissured by desert air and ancient longing. She belongs to the poignant songs of yesteryear movies that linger in the pan-Indian collective consciousness. She belongs to all those hosts who have welcomed her into their literatures and have sought to recreate her in their respective tongues. She belongs to women down the ages who have been inspired by her transgressive love. She belongs to seekers everywhere who know that disruptive yearning of which she sings with such pain and candor. And she belongs here, in these compelling verses by a translator who offers us a Mira of vulnerability and power. A Mira who detonates into scorching verse, but is also capable of simply being stunned into "garble".

Slippery and ungraspable, yet always our love-stained contemporary, Mira sings on.

—Arundhathi Subramaniam

Introduction

The classical Indian singer Lakshmi Shankar sang a concert in the sanctuary at St. John's Church, Berkeley, in August 1985. It was the same 1950s-era circular altar hall that had sheltered refugees, war resistors and worshippers. Accompanied by the two small drums called *tabla*, and a *tambura* with its five-string winding drone, she gave the first half of the evening to the hauntingly difficult, wide-ranging *khyal* of North India. After intermission, seated with the *swaramandala*, a small string instrument on her lap, she sang a series of *bhajan*, lighter and more popular in style though not in emotion. This was likely the first time I felt the lyrics of Mirabai slide like greased lightning through the body of an audience.

Friends at Shambhala Bookstore told me customers had come in asking for Indian poetry. The United States had designated 1985 "Festival of India," and for a moment Chola Dynasty bronze figures—cool, symmetrical, achingly voluptuous—had become iconic. Nobody knew names of any poets though, except for Kabir. Could I suggest some books worth reading? Thinking it over, I wrote a small review suggesting that if you wanted to get close to India's popular poetry, sung on the streets, in temples or concert halls in local idiom, you should search out a concert by Lakshmi Shankar or one of the many other fine singers, not settle for the stiff or misleading translations I had seen. A bit of research would turn up captivating tapes. I began a list of artists, and envisioned a lineage of singers keeping Mirabai's songs alive for four hundred years, mostly without books.

In 1993, the poet Leslie Scalapino offered to publish a collection of my essays and translations from classical India. She read my short essay on Lakshmi Shankar and proposed that I translate a handful of Mirabai's lyrics so readers could glimpse them as poems. I told her my essay had dismissed the translations available, urging readers to track down records instead. With quiet tact Leslie persisted until I agreed to try a few songs. That is the origin story of this book.

My studies had been in Sanskrit, a more formal earlier language. Asking around, I got an introduction to someone who had studied literary Hindi, close to Mirabai's language and more vernacular, juicier in performative values, than the old language I'd studied. I was now living in Colorado and climbed the snow-covered hillside through Ponderosa pines to my collaborator's house several times a week. We set off to see what we could manage. We listened again and again to a cassette tape of Kishori Amonkar singing Mirabai's *bandish* or compositions. I began a quest for other singers who had recorded Mira, and gathered a small set of tapes provided largely by friends. The two of us managed six poems over the course of a month; we had a *padāvalī*, a collection of lyrics, but took our clues from the singers. Singers explore Mirabai's lyrics with great flexibility, far different than what you find in the manuscripts which must have been transcribed from oral performance over the past several centuries.

When my friend bowed out of further work, I located a local man who played *bansuri*, the Indian bamboo flute, and who offered Hindi lessons. He loaned me a *kosa* (dictionary of medieval North Indian languages), I tracked down more recorded music, and I continued to translate. Initially I was dubious, but each song offered a white-hot emotion, and at least one or two bright images I knew from Sanskrit poetry: rains, the moon, streets, bird life, courtyards, flowering trees, woodlands, river banks. These unfolded slowly, the longer I listened to the winding lyrics and repeated phrases of the singers.

After Shreemati Amonkar's tape, the recording that seized me was a single track on an old UNESCO album, compiled by Alain Daniélou in 1962. The singer, Nandan Prasad, sounds like he sits by a prickly, arid, little-traveled track in Rajasthan—

small folk instrument on his thigh, the occasional traveler or donkey kicking alkaline dust near his mouth—singing for small coins or to free the bottomless anguish of his heart. That desolate voice, free of embellishment, never left me. It echoes through the voice of Mirabai in this book.

Other translators have fixed on Mira's birth as a noble daughter destined for high marriage, her education in the palace of a Rajput warlord, the sumptuous furnishings, jewels, fabrics and food of a warrior clan. I scarcely detect those in her lyrics. The Mirabai I find rejected gems long ago, silk, silver or gold, chariots, and ruthless husbands, along with the terribly subservient role a woman played in the Rajput era. You will hear more than a hint of luxury in some of the highly produced, splendid recordings by Anuradha Paudwal or Lata Mangeshkar. These embellish Mira's lyrics with simulated waterfalls, rhythmic clopping horse hooves, electric sitars, and reverb flutes. I find it all gorgeous. For better or worse, my Mirabai strikes a different string: desolate, solitary, thirsty, grief stricken; then an abrupt outbreak of ecstasy, shivery and acutely erotic.

Once I got to know the *thumri* singer Vidya Rao, she deepened the portrait I had of Mirabai, revealing a youthful vulnerability along with a later, desolate tone, seasoned by time. Vidya can shift the bare lyrics from one song style to another, changing their mood, their emotional color. Unbearable longing turns to teasing, almost a taunt, and back again on a note. I won't forget one night, Kartik Purnima, under a December moon in Delhi, hearing that ecstatic, defiant voice in a small park, as Vidya sang to a fluttering drum and the whinny of sinew on the *sarangi* that shadowed her.

For this set of eighty poems, I have hewn to Mirabai's spare, almost austere lyrics, and tried to convey the passion of Nandan Prasad, Kishori Amonkar, and Vidya Rao, a passion sometimes muffled, sometimes scraped raw. My debt to these three, and to Leslie Scalapino who years ago pressed me to translate, is incalculable.

—Andrew Schelling

Songs of Mirabai

paga bāndha ghūmgharyām nācyārī

Binding my ankles with silver
I danced—
people in town called me crazy.
She'll ruin the clan
said my mother-in-law,
and the prince
had a cup of venom delivered.
I laughed as I drank it.
Can't they see?
Body and mind aren't something to lose,
the Dark One's already seized them.
Mira's lord can lift mountains,
he is her refuge.

helī mhāmsūm hari bini

Friend, without that Dark raptor
I could not survive.
Mother-in-law shrills at me,
her daughter sneers,
the prince stumbles about in a permanent
          fury.
They've bolted the door
and mounted a guard.
But who could abandon the love
wakened through uncounted lifetimes?
The Dark One is Mirabai's lord,
who else could
          slake her desire?

mhāre dere ājyo

Come to my bedroom,
I've scattered fresh buds on the couch,
perfumed my body.
Birth after birth I am your servant,
sleep only with you.
Mira's lord does not perish—
one glimpse of the Dark One
   is all she requests.

māī mhārī hari hūm

Sister, the Dark One won't speak to me.
Why does this useless body keep breathing?
Another night gone
and no one's lifted my gown.
He won't speak to me.
Years pass, not a gesture.
They told me
he'd come when the rains came,
but lightning pierces the clouds,
the clock ticks until daybreak
and I feel the old dread.
Slave to the Dark One,
Mira's whole life is a long
night of craving.

mhāne cākara rākhāmjī

I am your slave.
Bind me in tethers, Mira's your slave.
She wakes up at dawn,
sits in the garden,
haunts the pathways of Vrindavan forest
making up ballads.
Fever, memory, craving,
birth after birth they come with me.
I slip on a saffron robe
hoping to see you.
Yogins come to Vrindavan to know oneness,
hermits perform terrible spells,
holy men come to sing gospels—
but Mira is deeper, lord,
and more secret.
She waits with a ruined heart every night
by the river
just for a glimpse.

sāmvariyo rangà rāchām rānā

He has stained me,
the color of raven he's stained me.
Beating a clay
two-headed drum at both ends
like a nautch girl I dance
before sadhus.
Back in town I'm called crazy,
drunkard, a love slut—
they incited the prince
who ordered me poisoned
but I drained the cup without missing a step.
Mira's lord is the true prince,
he stained her the color of raven,
birth after birth
she is his.

thāmne kāmī kami bol sunāvā

Dark Friend, what can I say?
This love I bring
from distant lifetimes is ancient,
do not revile it.
Seeing your elegant body
I'm ravished.
Visit our courtyard, hear the women
singing old hymns.
On the square I've laid
out a welcome of teardrops,
body and mind I surrendered ages ago,
taking refuge
wherever your feet pass.
Mira flees from lifetime to lifetime,
your virgin.

bhaja mana charana kamval

O Mind,
praise the lotus feet that don't perish!
Consider all things
on heaven and earth—and their doom.
Go off with pilgrims, undertake fasts,
wrangle for wisdom,
trek to Varanasi to die,
what's the use?
Arrogant body just withers,
phenomenal world is a coy parakeet
that flies off at dusk.
Why throw a hermit robe over your
            shoulders—
yellow rag yogins
are also bewildered,
caught every time in the birth snare.
Dark One, take this girl for your servant.
Then cut the cords and
set her free.

muraliyā bājā jamanā tīr

Down by Jamuna River a flute!
O ruined heart,
what is conviction
that the notes of a flute can dissolve it?
Dark waters, dark trousers
and Krishna darker than ever—
one bamboo flute note
so pure it drives Mira out of her mind.
Lord, this stumbling body,
      free it from torment.

jogī mata jā mata jā

Yogin, don't go,
at your feet a slave girl has fallen.
She lost herself
on a tangled path of romance and worship,
no one to guide her.
Now she's built
an incense and sandalwood pyre
she begs you to light it.
Dark One, don't go—
when only cinder remains
rub my ash over your body.
Mira asks, Dark One,
            can flame twist upon flame?

jogī mhāmne darasa diyām

Yogin, a single glimpse
and I'd be exultant.
But life on this crazy planet is torment,
day and night torment.
Mad, raked by separation,
drifting from country to country—
look at Mira's black hair
      it's turned white.

akhayām tarasā darasana pyāsī

Hungry eyes and I
crave him—
O friend, days shuttle past
while I rage out my lyric heart
on the highway.
A cuckoo up on a perch
torments my ear with its song.
Ugly words come from the citizens, they
            make
me the butt of their jokes.
Thus Mira is sold on the market,
into the hands of her Dark One,
birth after birth.

mhām giradhara āgām nācyārī

Dancing before him!
To whirl and to spin!
charming his artistic passions
testing old urges—
O Dark One beloved, I bind on my anklets,
true love is drunk.
Worldly shame! family decorum!
who needs such virtues?
Not for an instant, one eyeblink,
do I forget him—
he has seized me and stained me,
that Dark One.

jagamām jīvanā thorā

Life on this planet is fragile,
why take up a burden?
From mother and father
come birth,
but from the font of creation comes karma.
People waste life,
heaping up merit like they're buying and
            selling—
it's pointless.
I sing out the raptures
of Hari, go into passions with sadhus,
nothing disturbs me.
Mira says—it's your power Dark One,
but it's me who crosses
the limits.

barajī rī mhām syām bínā na rahyām

My Dark One,
they've placed him off limits—
but I won't live without him.
Delighting in Hari,
coming and going with sadhus,
I wander beyond reach of the world's snare.
Body is wealth
but I just give it away—
this head was long ago taken.
Full of rapture
Mira flees the jabbering townsfolk,
going for refuge
to what cannot perish—
her Dark One.

nīndarī āvām na sārām rāt

Another night without sleep,
thrashing about
until daybreak.
Friend, once I rose
from a luminous dream, a vision
that nothing dispels.
Yet this writhing, tormented self
cries out to meet ·
her Lord of the outcast.
Gone mad, gone crazy,
mind and senses confused with unspoken
        secrets—
Oh the Dark One
holds life and death in his hands,
he knows Mira's anguish.

bādala dekhā jharī

Clouds—
I watched as they ruptured,
ash black and pallid I saw mountainous
            clouds
split and spew rain
for two hours.
Everywhere water, plants and rainwater,
a riot of green on the earth.
My lover 's gone off
to some foreign country,
sopping wet at our doorway
I watch the clouds rupture.
Mira says, nothing can harm him.
This passion has yet
to be slaked.

rī mhām baithyām jāgām

Friend,
though the world sleeps
the abandoned go sleepless.
From inside the palace
counting the planets
someone threads teardrops onto a necklace.
The abandoned go sleepless.
Night has suddenly
vanished and Mira,
Mira has missed the hour of pleasure,
missed the Dark One who
        eases her pain.

aīī lagan lagāi

You pressed Mira's seal of love
then walked out.
Unable to see you
she's hopeless,
tossing in bed—gasping her life out.
Dark One, it's your fault—
I'll join the yoginis,
I'll take a blade to my throat in Banaras.
Mira gave herself to you,
you touched her intimate seal
and then left.

sāmvaro mhāro prīta

Dark One
all I request is a portion of love.
Whatever my defects,
you are for me an ocean of raptures.
Let the world cast its judgements
nothing changes my heart—
a single word from your lips is sufficient—
birth after birth
begging a share of that love.
Mira says, Dark One—enter the penetralia,
you've taken
this girl past the limits.

cālām vāhī desa

Go! Go to that land
where a glimpse of the Dark One
is had.
Give me the word,
I'll wear a red sari,
give me the word, I'll dress in hermit rags;
one word, I'll lace pearls
through the part in my hair,
or scatter my braids into dreadlocks.
Mira's lord rules the true court,
she says, go,
go where he dwells.
Then heed the songs of your
king.

naimda nahim āvai

Another night
sleepless,
tossing in bed,
reaching for someone not there.
Tossed darkness
life wasted
a tossed mind convulsing all night.
Another night sleepless and then,
the bright dawn.

mero bero lagājyo pār

Guide this little boat
over the waters,
what can I give you for fare?
Our mutable world holds nothing but grief,
bear me away from it.
Eight bonds of karma
have gripped me,
the whole of creation
swirls through eight million wombs,
through eight million birth-forms we flicker.
Mira cries, Dark One
take this little boat to the far shore,
put an end to coming
and going.

píyā ab para ājyo mere

Remember our pledge,
that you'd come to my cottage?
I'm strung out,
I stare down the road
and strain for a glimpse of you.
The hour we set
came and departed.
I sent a messenger girl
but Dark One, you tossed out the message
and deflowered the girl.
Days I don't see you are torment,
Mira knows you're with
somebody else.

barasām rī badariyā sāvan rī

Thick overhead
clouds of the monsoon,
a delight to this feverish heart.
Season of rain,
season of uncontrolled whispers—the Dark
      One's returning!
O swollen heart,
O sky brimming with moisture—
tongued lightning first
and then thunder,
convulsive spatters of rain,
then wind chasing the summertime heat.
Mira says Dark One,
I've waited,
it's time to take my songs
into the street.

sāmvalíyā mhāro chāya

My lover 's shadow
falls on foreign terrain,
not a note
to say where to meet him.
I cropped my hair,
stripped off my jewels and my gown,
threw on this beggar's robe,
and it's your fault.
My lover's shadow darkens
some other country
while I wear out my feet on the roads.
When Shyam left her bed
Mira's life became wreckage,
a ruin from
birth.

them mata barajām māi rī

Don't block my way, friend,
I'm joining the sadhus.
The Dark One's image sits in my heart,
now nothing gives solace.
O the citizens sleep,
their world groggy with
ignorance,
but I hold vigils all night.
Who understands these dark passions?
Wet with Shyam's love,
how could I sleep?
When it rains
does anyone drink from the gutter?
Mira says, Friend,
take this lost child.
At midnight she goes out half mad
to slake her thirst
at his fountain.

bidha bidhanā rī nyārām

Crooked fate,
crooked decree!
Look at the gentle-eyed deer
condemned
to wander the badlands.
It's crooked! A bright colored heron
that speaks with a rasp
while the articulate
cuckoo is charcoal!
Mira says look around you,
it's twisted—
thieves sit like kings
and our ablest scholars flee into exile.
Even the beggars of God
are made outlaw.

kāmī mhāro janama bārambār

Why life,
why again,
and what reason birth as a woman?
Good deeds in former lives they say.
But—
growth, cut, cut, decline—
life disappears second by second
and never comes back,
a leaf torn from its branch
twists away.
Look at this raging ocean of life forms,
swift, unappeasable,
everything caught in its tide.
O beloved, take this raft quickly
and lead it to shore.

lagan mhārī syām sūm lāgo

This is the seal of
dark love—
that my eyes should thrill with a vision.
My friend, I put on a bride's decorations
that my lover come quickly.
He is no
desolate man,
coming to birth only to perish.
I take the Dark One to bed!
He sates Mira's desire,
life after life
she awaits his arrival.

thāro rūpa dekhyām atakī

A glimpse of your body
has hooked me!
My family sets out their restraints
but I'll never forget
how the peacock-plumed dancer embraced
       me.
I'm loggy with Shyam,
people say—she meanders!
Yes Mira's hooked.
She goes into depths
where every secret is known.

sakhi mhāmro sāmariyā nai

Friend, I see
only the Dark One,
a dark swelling,
dark luster,
I'm fixed in trances of darkness.
Wherever my feet
touch soil I am dancing.
O Mira stares into darkness,
she ambles the back
country roads.

badalā re the jala bharyā ājyo

Come to me, cloud
bursting with water.
O secret friends
a drumming of rain, but listen—
the cuckoo is crying!
Thunderbolt music,
fresh wind,
ply after ply of cloud in the heavens.
Today my lover arrives
and I beg you to sing for him.
Mira's beloved
won't perish—
simply to look at him
is more wealth than
anyone needs.

josīrā ne lākh badhāyā

Ten thousand thanks
O astrologer
for announcing the Dark One's arrival!
Dizzy, ecstatic,
my soul goes into her bedroom.
Five companions converge,
five senses,
to give him unparalleled pleasure.
One glimpse of his form
dispels anguish,
all my erotic longings bear fruit.
Shyam, the ocean of pleasure,
has come into me.

nenām lobhām ātakām

Wolfish eyes fixed on the Dark One,
hungry, restless,
scouring every inch of his body.
When he came into view
smiling faintly,
lit up with moonlight,
I nearly collapsed by the door.
My family speaks of their plans
to restrain me
but my eyes flash through every obstruction.
Don't they know somebody's claimed me?
I lift to my forehead
every word uttered,
some ugly, some tender—
without the Dark One's approval
nothing survives.

jānyām na prabhu milana

It's a curse—
I don't even
know how to greet him,
when he slipped through the courtyard
I blew it.
Days and nights
searching for love on the roadways,
and when it comes through the
courtyard I'm sleeping.
Rejected, bewildered, on fire inside,
Mira wakes up
and everything's ruined.
Dark One it's slavery—
touch me once,
        you won't get away.

māī mhām govinda guna gānā

I will sing out his beauties!
So what if the king goes into a fury?
I can leave his domain
but anger the Dark One
where do I go?
Mira's in-laws delivered a cupful of poison
but I drank up ambrosia—
they concealed a black cobra in a wickerwork
       basket,
but I found the black precious stone.
O crazy Mira,
she's taken the Dark One
       off to her bridal bed!

Note: The "black stone" or *shalgrama* is a polished round rock found along the Gandaki River north of Patna, made smooth by millennia of water. It contains a fossil ammonite. Broken in half to reveal the paleontological miracle, Hindus worship it as a *murti* or image of Vishnu.

jānām re mohanā

I've tasted it, Drunk One,
tasted your passion!
I follow the path of romance and worship
and observe no other practice.
You plied me with sweets, now you give poison.
What is this teaching?
Mira's lord cannot perish,
      he befriends whomever he chooses.

ab to nibhāyām

Take my arm
and keep to your promise!
They call you the refugeless refuge,
they call you
redeemer of outcasts.
Caught in a riptide
in the sea of becoming
without your support I'm a shipwreck!
You reveal yourself age after age
and free the beggar
from her affliction.
Dark One, Mira is clutching your feet,
        at stake is your honor.

prabhu jī them kahām gayā

Having wet me with love
why did you leave?
You abandoned your unwavering consort
after lighting her lamp-wick;
call her a raft
set to drift on an ocean of craving.
Either way Mira's dead
      unless you return.

holī piyā bina lāgām rī khārī

How bitter is carnival day
with my lover off traveling.
O desolate town,
night and day wretched,
my small bed in the attic lies empty.
Rejected and lost
in his absence, stumbling under
the pain.
Must you wander
from country to country? It hurts me.
These fingers ache
counting the days you've been gone.
Spring arrives
with its festival games,
the chiming of anklets, drumbeats and flute,
          a sitar—
yet no beloved visits my gate.
What makes you forget?
Here I stand begging you, Dark One
don't shame me!
Mira comes to embrace you
birth after birth
          still a virgin.

acche mīthe cākh cākh

The plums tasted
sweet to the unlettered desert-tribe girl,
but what manners! To chew into each!
She was ungainly,
low-caste, ill mannered and dirty,
but the god took the
fruit she'd been sucking.
Why? She knew how to love.
She might not distinguish
splendor from filth
but she'd tasted the nectar of passion.
Might not know any Veda,
but a chariot swept her away.
Now she frolics in heaven, insatiably
bound to her god.
The Lord of Fallen Fools, says Mira,
will save anyone
who can practice rapture like that.
I myself in a previous birth
was a cow-herding girl
at Gokul.

tero maram nahim pāyo re

Yogin, I did not touch
your intimate secret.
Taking a mystical posture I sat
in a cave,
beads at my throat, limbs pasted with ash.
I had raptures over the Dark One, but no—
I never touched
his imperishable secret.
What Mira obtains
has been written by fate.

jogíyārī prītarī

Take a yogin
for lover, get nothing but grief.
He beguiles you with intimate whispers, all
          worthless.
Sister, he plucks your flower
like a sprig of jasmine,
then pulls on his robe and is gone.
Mira says, Dark One,
I saw you once,
          but tonight I'm an utter wreck.

ho gaye syāma dūija ke candā

Over the trees
a crescent moon glides.
The Dark One has gone to dwell in Mathura.
Me, I struggle, caught in a love noose
and yes,
Mira's lord can lift mountains
but today his passion
          seems distant and faint.

koī kachū kahe mana lāgā

Let them gossip.
This mind never wavers.
Love fixes my mind on that enchanter of
      minds
like sorcery fixes on gold.
Birth after birth lost in sleep
until hearing the teacher's
word I awoke.
Mother, father, household, tribe—
snapped like a thread!
Mira's lord can lift mountains,
he has awakened her.

māī mhāre supnā mām

In my dream, sister,
the Lord of the Downtrodden wed me.
Deities danced in attendance,
fifty-six million,
the Dark One was groom in my dream.
In my dream were arched wedding gateways,
a clasping of hands, sister.
In a dream
the Lord of the Downtrodden
married Mira and took her to bed.
Good fortune from previous births
comes to fruit.

jogīya ne kahajyo

Take my message
to that wandering yogin,
tell him I've worn out my fingers
counting the days,
           the time has arrived.

Matting my hair into dreadlocks
I'll strip off my gown,
wrap up in tatters
and take the left-hand path of the wizards.
Mystical earrings, charmed necklace,
ratty old beggar's robe,
I'll deck myself out,
           skull in my hand for a food bowl.

I'll wander savage countries
because you, the protector of girls,
knocking around faraway cities these days,
give no protection.
Mystical earrings, anchorite beads,
dead man's skull in my hand,

O crazy yogini, Mira—
      roaming the ages, hunting you down!

Time and again
you promised you'd come when the rains
      came,
a handful of
pledges all worthless.
Look at my fingers
calloused from counting the days.
I've even turned yellow with anguish,
a grisly look
      for a child.

Mira the slave girl
gave her god prayers,
she might as well give him
      body and mind.

maim to teri sarana parī

Refuge in you, Dark One,
you alone
know how to save me.
A girl possessed,
I shamble through the sixty-eight places
of pilgrimage
but haven't the wit to know failure.
Hear my cry, O Murari—
nothing on earth
looks like it's "mine."
Mira gave you her trust, now it's your move.
Spring her from this noose
        we call "world."

he mā barī barī ankhiyan vāro

Listen, friend,
the Dark One laughs
and scours my body with ravenous eyes.
Eyebrows are bows,
darting glances are arrows that pierce
       a wrecked heart.

You will heal
I'll bind you with magical diagrams
and crush drugs
for a poultice.
But if it's love that afflicts you
       my powers are worthless

Sister, how can I heal?
I've already
crushed sandalwood paste,
tried witchcraft—charms and weird spells.
Wherever I go
his sweet form is laughing inside me.
Tear open these breasts

you'll see a torn heart!
Unless she enclasps her dark lover
how can Mira
       endure her own body?

nahim sukhā bhāvai thāmro desalaro

Your colorful kingdom
just bores me.
Among your subjects no seekers, O Prince,
only trash.
These people are abject!
Prince Ratan Singh,
I strip off my jewelry,
throw down my bangles,
wipe off eye-black and rouge.
I shake the barrettes from my hair.
Why? Mira has found
a lord who lifts mountains,
a lover who fills her
         completely.

ranaji mhane ya badnami

This infamy, O my Prince,
is delicious!
Some revile me,
others applaud,
I simply follow my incomprehensible road.
A razor thin path
but you meet some good people,
a terrible path but you hear a true word.
Turn back?
Because the wretched stare and see nothing?
O Mira's lord is noble and dark,
and slanderers
rake only themselves
        over the coals.

dari gayo manamohana

Snared me—
and now the Enchanter has vanished!
An overhead tree, a cuckoo is singing,
people play amorous games.
For me it's a death chill,
the Enchanter bewitched me and vanished.
I stumble through woodlands,
fevered, rejected.
What's left but a blade for my
throat at Varanasi?
O the Caster of Spells does not perish.
But look at Mira,
        she dies like a slave.

payi vbina rahyām na jāyām

Unable to live since
he left,
heart, body, breath given up.
Day and night a
ghost on the highway
lured by remembrance of beauty.
Lifting her throat
Mira the slave girl cries out:
       Fetch me home!

bhaī hom bāvarī sun ke bāmsurī

Gone mad, sister,
my lover's departed, but listen!
a flute!
O whirling senses,
heart reckless and tangled and mad!
What sort of flute
works this uncanny priestcraft?
Even Mira's lord can't untangle this snare,
the power of seven
        musical notes.

mere priyatama pyāre rāma kūm

I scrawl
endless letters and send them
to Shyam.
Why does he hold this
deliberate silence?
Night after night no reply.
Sweeping the walk every day,
wrecking my eyesight
watching the road,
when will he come, that Dark One?
We were lovers once, in a
previous life.

āvo manamohana jī

O sweet tongued Enchanter,
I was a child.
You paid no attention to my
little girl love,
then you vanished.
Bewitched, jerked here and there,
I stumble about,
contradictions eating my heart.
Don't you get it? Mira is yours.
One word, sweet tongued Enchanter,
I'll tell everyone.
I'll beat it out
on my drum.

karanām suni syām merī

Hear my plea, Dark One, I am
your servant,
a vision of you has driven me mad.
Separation eats at my limbs.
Because of you
I'll become a yogini and ramble
from city to city
scouring the hidden quarters—
pasted with ash, clad in a deerskin
my body wasting
to cinder.
I'll circle from forest to forest
wretched and howling—
O Unborn, Indestructible,
come to your beggar!
Finish her pain and touch her
with pleasure!
This coming and going will end,
says Mira,
with me clasping your
        feet forever.

saiyām tum vini nīnda na āvaī

Dark One, how can I sleep?
Since you left my bed
the seconds drag past like epochs,
each moment
a new torrent of pain.
I am no wife,
no lover comes through the darkness—
lamps, houses, no comfort.
On my couch
the embroidered flowers
pierce me like thistles,
      I toss through the night.

Yet who would believe my story?
That a lover
bit my hand like a snake,
and the venom bursts through

and I'm dying?

I hear
the peacock's faraway gospel,
the nightingale's love song,
the cuckoo.
Thickness on thickness folds through the
     sky,
clouds flash with rain.
Dark One, is there no love
in this world
that such anguish continues?
Mirabai waits for a
     glance from your eye.

mīrām lāgau ranga harī

The Dark One's love-stain
is on her,
other ornaments
Mira sees as mere glitter.
A mark on her forehead,
a bracelet, some prayer beads,
beyond that she wears only
        her conduct.

Make-up is worthless
when you've gotten truth from a teacher.
O the Dark One has
stained me with love,
and for that some revile me,
others give honor.
I simply wander the road of the sadhus
        lost in my songs.

Never stealing,
injuring no one,
who can discredit me?
Do you think I'd step down from an
        elephant
to ride on the haunch
        of an ass?

letām letām rāma nāma re

Shame would kill
these people
if anyone heard them speak the true word.
They dash
from here to there in the village
but complain they're too tired to visit a
            temple.
A fight breaks out
they storm off to watch it;
a busker starts jesting,
a whore dances,
the townsfolk sit laughing for hours.
But Mira sits somewhere else,
at the lotus feet
            of her Dark One.

prabhu so milana kaise hoy

When can I meet
the Dark Lord?
Caught up in duties fifteen
hours a day,
nine hours absent in sleep.
Human birth, says Mira,
is precious
but we get it and waste it.
Give yourself to the Dark One,
fate never swerves
        from its course.

yā vraja mem kachū dekhyo rī

O I saw witchcraft tonight
in the region of Braj.
A milking girl going her rounds,
a pot on her head,
came face to face with the Dark One.
My friend, she is babbling,
can no longer say "buttermilk."
Come get the Dark One, the Dark One!
A pot full of Shyam!
In the overgrown lanes
of Vrindavan forest
the Enchanter of Hearts fixed his
eye on this girl,
then departed.
Mira's lord is hot, lovely
and raven—
tonight she saw witchcraft
at Braj.

koī syāma manohara lyorī

Stumbling about,
a clay pot on her head,
the word for
buttermilk gone from her tongue—
Who will take darkness, the Taker of Hearts?
Come take the taker, the taker!
The milking girl's lost in a
dark body seizure,
          her mouth full of garble.

māī rī mhā kiyām govindām mol

Sister,
I went into market
and picked up the Dark One.
You whisper
as though it were shameful,
I strike my drum and declare it in public.
You say I paid high,
I say I weighed it out on the scales,
it was cheap.
Money's no good here,
I traded my body, I paid with my life!
Dark One, give Mira a glance,
we struck a bargain
          lifetimes ago.

papaiyā re piva kī vānī

Dreadful cuckoo
who said you could sing about love?
A girl like me
might twist off your wings in a fury,
rip out your beak,
pour salt on the wounds.
The Beloved is mine,
  your song to him is an outrage!

Yet if today
the Dark One showed up
I'd weep with delight at your tune,
you'd be my companion,
I'd paint gold
  on your beak.

Look,
I've drafted a letter,
fly to him quickly,
say the girl he rejected's quit eating,
won't sleep,
goes into fits—
that every dawn Mira sings
to her Dark One,
Come quickly,
        your absence destroys me.

kina sang khelūm holī

Terrible solitude
festival day
now that he's gone.
Damn these rubies and pearls,
I'll string devotional beads
at my throat.
And here's an old hermit cloak—
now that food and house
are distasteful
it matches my feelings.
What makes me like this?
It's a riddle.
You take me to bed
then go off and fuck
some other girl.
Does she have you under her spell
that you can't even write me?
Mira's a bundle of nerves in your absence.
Look at her,
an unwatered weed when the
Dark One's away,
        she wilts in the rubble.

jāgo bamsīvāre lalanā

Wake up,
my lover of women,
my amorous fluteplayer,
night has fled,
it is dawn.
Shutters bang open in house after house.
Hear the bracelets
chiming together
as *gopis* strain at their butter churns.
Wake up, it is dawn,
gods and men
throng through the doorways;
cowherding boys,
their little hands stuffed with bread and butter,
drive cattle to pasture.
Wake up! Mira says,
The fluteplayer will save you,
but you must come
            seeking refuge.

māī mero mohane mana haryo

Sister, the Enchanter
has stolen my heart.
Where can I go,
what can I do,
he took the breath from my lungs.
I'd gone to the river
a jug on my head
when a figure rose through the darkness.
Sister, it cast a sorcerer's noose
and it bound me.
What the world calls virtue suddenly vanished.
I performed a strange rite.
Mira may be a slave, Sister,
but she herself
            chose whom to sleep with.

kahām kahām jāūm tere sāth

Dark One
where are we going?
The groves and pathways of Vrindavan forest
had folded around us,
abruptly the Enchanter embraced me.
He drank up my curds
and shattered the earthenware pot.
With a blaze
of fragrance and darkness
he snatched my earthenware vessel
and broke it apart.
Where are we going, Dark One,
why this confusion?
You come and you go through Gokul,
rejecting my gifts,
yet you are the lord
          who heaps birth upon birth.

syāma bina duhkha pāvām sajanī

He's gone
friend, and I suffer.
Whatever I cling to dissolves.
This drifting world's a
turbulent cauldron,
it leaves nomads of truth without shelter.
Seekers get mocked,
people act rashly,
they fling themselves into infernos
and no one gets free—
just the churning
of eight million wombs.
Groping,
at every turn twisting,
missing the passage towards freedom.
Mira says, Dark One,
we call refuge in you
            "the beyond."

āj mhāmro sādhu janano sangare

Good fortune
my Prince,
today I went among sadhus!
Coming and going
I tasted their splendor four times.
But Goddess cults—
shun them—
they'll wreck your devotion!
Forget the fashionable visits
of pilgrims,
Banaras and Ganges are found
at a holy man's feet.
Don't mock the seekers,
you'll be dipped
in a hell pool,
go crippled or blind.
Yes Mira's lord can lift mountains,
today she covered her body
with dust from a
            holy man's feet.

papaiyā mhārī kab rau

Why this impulse
to hurt me, O cuckoo?
I was in my own
hut asleep
when you cried out a love song,
rubbing salt in the wound.
There you sat
high on a tree branch
singing from deep
          in your throat.

bhīje mhāmro dāmvan cīr

Out in a downpour
in a sopping wet
skirt.
And you have gone to a distant country.
Unbearable heart,
letter after letter
just asking when,
my lord, when
        do you come back?

mīltā jājyo ho jī gumānī

Come, O aloof one
a glimpse of
your body has caught me.
My name?
Call me the girl
who separation drove mad.
Night and day there's a fish
thrashing
next to the water,
servant Mira dies at your feet—
and she calls you the
        Giver of Joy.

giradhara rīsānā kaun gunām

What is this anger
from one who lifts mountains?
Did I fail you,
          affront you?
Dropping through womb
after womb,
servant Mira returns,
calling your name
          every time.

jhatakyo merī cīr

Murari yanked
at my skirt,
the clay pot of indigo bounced
from my head,
my sari snagged on my
nose ring,
hair knot slipped loose,
earrings got tangled—
the Dark One makes love an art of
enchantment.
I lower my head
        to his feet.

premanī premanī premanī re

Passion,
passion's the dagger that
savaged this heart.
I'd gone to Jamuna River
a gold pot on my head.
The Dark One tossed out a thread,
bound me,
and led me along.
O I see darkness,
unspeakable beauties,
       now I see omens.

mhāro mana sāmvaro

O creatures of earth,
I wiped out ten million ignorant deeds
by calling on Shyam,
his name revolves in my heart.
Countless vile births
countless ancient depravities
drained like a
cup of sweet juice.
Mira's lord does not perish,
he wipes out ill karma,
      he sweetens body and mind.

matavāro bādara

Drunk, turbulent clouds
roll overhead
but they bring from the Dark One
no message.
Listen!
the cry of a peacock,
a nightingale's faraway ballad,
a cuckoo!
Lightning
flares in the darkness,
a rejected girl shivers,
thunder, sweet wind and rain.
Lifetimes ago
Mira's heart went with the Dark One.
Tonight in her solitude
infidelity spits
     like a snake—

Mirabai's Life, Legend, & Song

Mirabai, born to a regal family in the district of Rajasthan, lived during the first half of the sixteenth century. Along with Kabir, whose life overlapped hers, she is known across South Asia and abroad, largely through the performance of singers. Mahatma Gandhi thought she exemplified *satyagraha*, civil disobedience, and spread her fame through twentieth century India. Films have memorialized her life, and thousands of recordings have appeared. In both India and the West people describe her verse as "devotional," an adequate but limited translation of bhajan, a style of singing typically used for Mirabai's *bandish*, or lyrics. Scholars have examined the lyrics in theological terms, or draw on them to illuminate religious ideas, feminist impulses, caste, or other social issues. These approaches catch some element of Mirabai's art but never explain her electrifying effect, or the way her lyrics reach across languages and excite people who do not share her history, culture, or religion.

When you listen to the songs, Mirabai strikes you as alternating acutely painful desire with enviable rapture. She is fearless and defiant, heroic in the solitude of her song. Her peers are not just the mystics of old India. Nor are her peers the troop of religious saints who emerge through history to express spiritual visions in verse. Mirabai belongs to a wider company: poets who during times of turbulent politics, war, and frightful unrest, cast everything into the fire, in order to lead an unblinkingly honest life. Among poets, she has much in common with the Trobairitz—women troubadors of 13th century Provence—with Sor Juana Inés de la Cruz of New Spain; or with the heartbreaking, misunderstood Ono no Komachi of ninth century Heian Japan. In the twentieth century she stands with Anna Akhmatova and Marina Tsetaeva. All of them women in conflict with the powerful figures of their day, each of them salted with fire.

Most details of Mirabai's life come clothed in a mix of fact and legend. The following account follows the most widely held beliefs.

The date given for Mirabai's birth is 1498. She was born into a Rajput or warrior clan, the Rathors, who ruled Rajasthan's city of Merta and its surrounding villages. A great grandfather on her father's side, Jodhaji, founded the city of Jodhpur, still one of Rajasthan's centers of handcraft, industry and trade. Mira's own father, Ratnasingh, held a dozen towns, including Kudki, site of the palace where Mira was raised.

It was a troubled era. Warrior clans of great

ruthlessness fought over territory and trade. They regarded one another with too much mistrust and enmity to unite against the Moghul rulers who held the Empire in Delhi. But threatened by outside legions, they had enough centralized identity to forge brief alliances and fight fiercely, leaving them unconquered by the Moghuls.

Unsteady alliances, hot tempers, brutal feuds, and rigid pride kept everyone edgy. If you visit Rajasthan, stop by one of the old Rajput palaces. Ask to see its armory of weapons. Blades, cudgels, cutters, clubs, lances, and huge two-blade scissors made to open an enemy's entrails. You get an idea how tenaciously warfare gripped the imaginations of the martial clans, and with how little mercy they carved up the territories.

The Rajputs of Mirabai's day exacted a strict loyalty from wives, sisters, and daughters. Among the ruling families, which impressed an exaggerated sexual modesty on women, marriage had a principal objective: to secure a military alliance. Following custom, Mira's family married her into a neighboring clan, the Sisodiya Rajputs of Mewar, likely to stabilize local politics or avert a blood feud. As a princess being readied for a politically consequential marriage, Mira would have been tutored in a variety of arts. Music, poetry, dance; perhaps theatre. Judging by how well her songs fit with India's long tradition of poetry, one suspects some of the old Sanskrit texts with their formalized love poetry came to her. As for the martial arts, she would have known them—if only from the far-out arrogant swagger of the warriors she grew up with.

A traditional story tells how, as a child, Mira answered the palace gate to give food to a *sadhu*, a religious almsman. He has never been identified, but is reputed to have whispered a few words in her ear, then pushed into her fist a tiny likeness of Krishna. She treasured the gift. In a few songs she speaks of receiving the words of a guru. No account has surfaced of her having taken a teacher or having sought religious instruction. Tradition ascribes to those whispered words all the training she needed.

One day Mira, seeing a wedding procession outside the palace, pestered her mother. Who was she to marry? When would the wedding take place? A Rajasthani girl of her pedigree knew this to be the event for which childhood prepares her. Her mother in jest or exasperation pointed to the little Krishna. "To him. Krishna will be your groom." From that moment Mira regarded Krishna as her beloved. She addressed him by the name *Śyām*, or *Shyam*.

Shyam is the word for a particular tone of reflective blue-black. "Dark One" is a common translation. Paintings and murals of Krishna (another word for black) show his skin glistening, radiating an aura of midnight blue. Sometimes I think *raven* a fitting term, since their wings have an iridescence that flashes blue in dry sunlight.

At twenty years of age Mira was wed to a man named Bhojraj, son of a renowned warrior, Rana Sanga. By Rajput law, she was now more than a wife, and in effect belonged to the Sisodiya clan. She'd become their property, an asset like a fine mare or prize elephant. In a few songs she twists things around and speaks of being sold off at market. It is no simple metaphor. She felt the raw degradation of being bartered or sold.

The Sisodiya creed was Shakta (*Śakta*)—worshippers of the *Śakti* or goddess in the manifestation of Kali. The family expected Mirabai to assume their religion. More specifically, by the Rajasthani institution of *suhag*, she was to discharge her religious duties through unquestioning service to her husband. Her new life would include devotion to household deities and unswerving obedience to her in-laws. She simply refused. One account says on entering the new palace she dutifully touched her mother-in-law's feet, but walked past the image of Kali. She was on intimate terms with the true Lord. How could she bow to a block of stone?

Compounding the indignity, Mira insisted that Shyam, pledged to her lifetimes ago, was her true husband. Was she repeating her mother's words? Or something the *sadhu* had whispered to her as a child? Shyam, the dark-skinned, adolescent, mischievous, flute-playing form of Krishna, adored in rural villages and markets. He was quite remote from the guidelines of the priests.

Stories say Mira refused to sleep with her husband. Details about Bhojraj don't really exist. Only in recent years have scholars located a historical figure. Probably a bit weak-minded for a warrior he barely shows up in the Mirabai stories. It's thought he died on the battlefield not long after the wedding.

Mira rejected the conventions of widowhood. She took to singing and dancing, dedicating songs to Shyam. Her songs plead and adore, cry out to him, scold, weep, and sometimes break into cries of sexual ecstasy. Ignoring the stringent behavior expected for widows, she would walk from the Sisodiya palace into town. She spent her days with mendicants and low-caste *bhaktas* (worshippers) in the market streets. Her in-laws were furious. Vikram Singh, a brother-in-law who succeeded his father as Rana—clan leader or prince—suspected Mirabai's *sadhu* friends for spies.

Vikram Singh's concern was not without ground. Wandering religious beggars were free to crisscross borders on pilgrimage, often unaccosted by local authorities. They made unlikely but occasionally skilled military informants. In later centuries the British used the *sadhu* or *pandita* for espionage and map making in Tibet and Central Asia. A fictional figure modeled on the Tibetan language scholar Sarat Chandra Das—who was also a British agent—is central to Rudyard Kipling's *Kim*. Vikram Singh went farther: he suspected Mirabai's songs held coded military information. After failing to subdue Mira by posting a guard at her door in the palace, Vikram Singh and his mother attempted three times to kill her.

First they had a drink delivered, telling her it was water sanctified by being poured over the feet of a Krishna image. They'd in fact laced it with poison. In one of her popular songs—*pad gunghru bandh*, the poem I open this collection with—Mira lightly sings that she "drained the cup" without missing a step in her dance. Her in-laws then sent her a wicker-basket of fruit, a black cobra under its lid. When Mira removed the lid in the serpent's place lay a *salgram*—one of the black fossil ammonites that turn up in the bed of the Gandaki River. Worshippers take the *salgram* as an emanation of Vishnu. In a final attempt on her life, Mira's in-laws forced her onto a bed of sharp spikes. The spikes as she lay on them turned into flower petals.

Three attempts on her life. Her admirers say three times Mira's god interceded. The more cold-eyed interpretation is that allies in the palace replaced each lethal substance with something inert. The day's politics were complex. Agents might have been in the palace. Mirabai would have been a precarious target. Her songs, her disregard for convention, her defense of the poor, had earned her notoriety in the region. One suspects her Rathor family ties remained in place too. No Rajput family would take assassination lightly.

Trust in god but keep your powder dry. Mira's god might keep a close eye on her but Mira knew the next step. She fled Sisodiya territory like a convict going over the wall. She took to the road on foot, left the pride and luxury, the calculating in-laws, the mediocre religion, and the stultifying life expected her as a widow.

For the remainder of her life she is said to have crisscrossed the roadways of Rajasthan and Gujarat, and other regions of North India, searching for Krishna wherever rumor placed him. In her songs, which draw on long-told stories of Krishna, Shyam is irresistibly adolescent. Breathing across the *bansuri*, a bamboo flute in his hand, he bewitches the cow-herding girls of the rural districts. They slip from their homes after dark, away from husbands and family duties, to enjoy a night of dancing, ecstatic song, and rapturous adulterous love. Mira calls Shyam by many names. Each illuminates some aspect of his character, or refers to a tale. Giradhar, Lifter of Mountains;[1] Manamohan, Enchanter of Hearts; Hari, the Abductor. Nothing quite prepares you for her undaunted pursuit. In Mirabai's poem, Shyam is more lover than god. Mostly he is a few leagues away, devastating her with his absence, tormenting her sleep with fears of infidelity.

Legends began to cluster around Mirabai. I think the reason is clear. Unlike other celebrated poets of her epoch who sing to a god—men like Surdas and Tulsidas—Mira's songs hold no theological arguments. She has no secret formula, there's no code to crack. Her songs are amorous, hungry, full of ecstasy, tossed with despair. Her songs never sound pious. She brings

1 - Robert Bly translates Giridhar as "the energy that lifts mountains," a contemporary, almost geological way of rendering the name. Lovely as it is, his term misses the way the name refers to a specific tale in the Krishna cycles. The people of Madhuban had angered old Vedic rain god Indra by abandoning him for the new Krishna sect. Indra angrily assailed the people with torrential rain and fierce lightning bolts. Krishna uprooted a mountain and lifted it, a cosmic umbrella, on one finger to protect his new followers and their cattle. Giridhar means "mountain lifter."

to life thousands of years of love poetry in India, giving a new insight. What she does is to sweep erotic urge into religious conviction. Or, she brings spiritual devotion into the body's sexual glands.

By her fiftieth year Mira had settled in Dwarka, a city in Gujarat. In Dwarka stands the Ranchhorji temple, one of India's four cardinal destinations of pilgrimage, the Arabian Sea beating against great stone pilings at its rear doors. In his small speculative biography, Herman Goetz suggests Mira set up a soup kitchen and hospice alongside the temple. Drawing on local stories, Goetz recounts how back in Sisodiya territory, the clan had suffered a number of devastating military reversals. One account says 13,000 women, learning their husbands had fallen in battle, collectively burned themselves on a pyre rather than suffer capture by enemy forces. Rumors circulated that the defeats had occurred as divine retribution for the clan's mistreatment of Mirabai. Confronted with discontent in their realm, Mira's in-laws decided to get her back, planning to manipulate her fame in order to shore up their rule. They sent a crew of Brahmins to Dwarka to fetch her.

The envoy located her at the soup kitchen by the temple. When she refused to return with them, the Brahmins threatened to starve themselves if she resisted. They knew Mirabai could not take on the burden of their deaths.

Faced with a return to the Sisodiya household, the wealth that held no interest, the title she'd rejected as useless, the ugly duties of a widowed princess, Mira requested a final night alone in the Ranchhorji temple, which housed an image of her god. In the morning when she did not emerge, the envoi forced the gates. What they found—draped over the feet of the stone Krishna—were Mirabai's robe and her hair.

Nobody knows how many songs Mira composed. Half a century ago Parashuram Chuturvedi, editing a careful edition of Mirabai's songs, cited a survey that found 5,197 with her name. Of these scholars regard three or four hundred as authentic, based on linguistic evidence. One way of looking at the works of a singer like Mirabai, however, is to regard her as a tradition, not so much a singular person with documented life events. She could be a spirit of rebellion that many singers manifest. Ranjit Hoskote, in his volume of Kashmiri poet Lal Ded, writes that Lalla's body is "the body of her work." Singers have placed Mirabai's name in new songs for centuries, adding to an ongoing, sustained lineage. Some call it the Mirabai tradition. I like the idea; it helps to sort out the huge number of songs. Yet I cannot let go of the unmistakable figure, the Mirabai who emerges with such clear personhood in so many of the songs. Someone once had to reside at the center of those wild lyrics.

A number of Mira's songs belong to the repertoire of any classical Hindustani singer today. They also feed an undiminished folk tradition. Wander the small villages, go into cities, sit at truck stop cafes; anywhere Krishna is recognized. You will hear Mira's poetry—in courtyards, on concert hall stages, along highways, in the markets, on popular radio. Like others, I have sat all night during the rainy season in a small smoke-darkened stone-block Rajasthan temple, while people sing Mirabai to a few finger cymbals, a harmonium, and a drum.

Mirabai's songs have been kept alive orally. Chronicles from the Ranchhorji temple at Dwarka show there once was a notebook or manuscript among its belongings. Oral tradition speaks of a companion named Lalita, a childhood maid of Mirabai's, who followed her into exile. Lalita faithfully transcribed the songs into a notebook. Whatever the origin of the Dwarka manuscript, it disappeared when a Moslem warlord plundered the temple in the seventeenth century. The earliest Mirabai manuscript is separated from her by 200 years. Hers has been a song tradition, five hundred years circulating from singer to singer.

Part of what makes her songs popular, urgent, and irrepressible, is the way their passion never feels more than a step or two from India's folk song. It also may be that in a country where, for most of history, writing has been the preserve of men, Mirabai is an archive curated by women.

There have been modern attempts to compile a scholarly edition. The standard is the *Mirambai ki Padavali*, by Parashuram Caturvedi. A revised edition came out in 1983. Caturvedi sets down lyrics to 202 songs he regards as likely to have been Mirabai's, another eighteen which he think possibly hers. Preparing my translations, I have worked mostly from Caturvedi's lyrics. As much as possible, though, I have gone directly to recordings, a few of which print lyrics. And to hear singers.

I certainly do not keep Caturvedi's order though. He grouped songs by raga, the musical modes they are traditionally associated with. Mirabai never did this. Since she was a singer, any order of songs would have been a daily performance, not a book's sequence.

Some lyrics may refer to events in Mirabai's life. Maybe these belong together, but I haven't placed them in an order that assumes them to be biographical. Mirabai was a refined and learned woman. She drew on both classical and folk traditions, literary and oral. She stands within a tradition of Indian love poetry that predates her, and which developed the particular use of imagery and established certain gestures and figures of speech. The tradition works with local plants, animals, weather patterns, family structures, musical instruments, geographies, and the performance arts of South Asia.

For my understanding of Mirabai's art, I resort every time to the singers. Recordings I keep to hand are by Kishori Amonkar, Lata Mangeshkar, M.S. Subhalakshmi, Lakshmi Shankhar, Anuradha Paudwal, and Vidya Rao. They hold what a printed text often does not: the delicate grief, the desolation, the intimate whimpers, the ecstatic calls, the notes that bend and dip. If you hope to know more, I urge you to go to the singers.

—Andrew Schelling
Colorado, February 2024

Glossary of Names, Places, and Terms

bhakta: Devotee, or lover of god. One might say "beggar" of God. Etymologically the word evokes a person who gives a portion to god.

bhakti: Devotion. The *bhakti marg* is the path of worship, *bhakti* poetry a verse of devotion. A populist reaction against tight control exercised by priests and ritual specialists, *bhakti* appeared in south India around the tenth century, took fire as a spiritual and cultural rebellion, then spread into the north. By Mirabai's day there existed many singers who drew from Hindu and Sufi traditions alike.

Braj: Region in east Rajasthan where Krishna spent his childhood among cowherds. Vrindavan forest lies here—where the Dark One played amorous games as a youth, and where Mirabai is said to have traveled in search of him when she fled her palace confines.

Gokul: Village of cowherding people on the banks of Jamuna (or Yamuna) River. Associated with the childhood of Krishna. It is here that the *gopis* (see following entry) fall in love with Krishna and become his beloved devotees.

gopi: Cow-herding girl. The *gopis* recklessly seek their god, whose midnight flute maddens them, drawing them from their homes and husbands, to dance and make love in the forest. Theirs is a circle dance, a perilous one because Krishna at their center is not husband but lover.

Hari: Seizer or Abductor: epithet of Krishna. The pious call on him to "seize away" their sins. The reckless *bhakta* cries for him to seize body, mind, and spirit entirely.

Jamuna (often written Yamuna) River: River in India, particularly associated in legend with Krishna.

Mathura: City along the Jamuna River in present-day Uttar Pradesh. Long associated with Krishna.

Murari: Slayer of Mura, epithet for Krishna drawn from legend in which the infant Krishna killed a demon, Mura, that had been terrorizing villagers around Gokul.

sadhu: Originally an archery term for an arrow that hits its mark: bulls-eye, or colloquially "right on," "wonderful." It now refers to a spiritual seeker who aims without distraction to hit the final goal of liberation. *Sadhus* undertake dramatic practices of asceticism. You can recognize their orange or saffron robes, begging bowls, and hair dreadlocked with cow-dung or crematory ash. Some use a skull for a food bowl. Some wear black robes.

Shyam: The Dark One, the Raven-Colored. Like the word *krishna*, this color denotes a glossy, lustrous black. In paintings it feels vibrant, in contrast to the unre-flective black, associated with Kali, which returns no light to your eye.

Varanasi (Angilicized as Banaras or Banares): India's holiest city, one of the longest continually inhabited places on earth. The aged, ill and infirm have for mil-lennia traveled to it to die, hoping to depart from one of the burning *ghats* or landings along the Ganges River. Orthodox Hindus believe that to die in Vara-nasi delivers you immediately to heaven. In Mirabai's day, special saw blades were available in the city, so people suffering spiritual despair could slice their own throats, assuring a trip to heaven or a congenial rebirth.

Veda: The ancient set of verse or *stotra*: praise poems, prayers, spells, riddles, and visions, dating to about 1700 B.C.E. Long before Mirabai's day, an entrenched priesthood had taken possession of the *Veda*, and claimed that their rituals formed the only legitimate spiritual path. *Bhakti* arose in response to dogmatic, literalist religion.

Vrindavan: Forested area closely associated with Krishna. Many temples have appeared over the centuries.

yogin, yogini: Sanskrit term for a practitioner of spiritual union, or *yoga*. The term gets applied to saints, devotees, anchorites, wizards, and sorcerers. *Yogin* is the masculine form, *yogini* the feminine. *Yogi* has become common English. Mirabai used a vernacular pronunciation *jogi*, or, when speaking of herself, *jogini*, the feminine noun.

Bibliography

Texts Used for this Edition

Caturvadi, Parashuram, ed. *Mirambai ki Padavali*. Allahabad: Hindi Sahitya Sammelan, 1973.

Prasad, Kalika. *Brihat Hindi Kosh*. Varanasi: Jnanamandala Editions, no date.

Shashi Prabha. *Miram Kosh*. Allahabad: Smriti Prakashan, 1974.

Singh, Neelima, ed. *Mira: Ek Antarang Parichaya*. Delhi: Saraswati Vihara, 1982.

English Translations and Accounts of Mirabai

Alston, A.J. *Devotional Poems of Miarabai*. Delhi: Motilal Banarsidas, 1980. Translations of all 202 poems from the *Mirabai ki Padavali*.

Bly, Robert and Jane Hirshfield. *Mirabai, Ecstatic Poems*. Boston: Beacon Press, 2004.

Goetz, Hermann. *Mira Bai, Her Life and Times*. Bombay:

Bharatiya Vidya Bhavan, 1966.

Hawley, John S. and J.M. Jurgenmeyer. *Songs of the Saints of India*. New York: Oxford University Press, 1988.

Levi, Louise Landes. *Sweet On My Lips: The Love Poems of Mirabai*. Brooklyn: Cool Grove Press, 1997.

Mirabai. (Comic book). Bombay: India Book House, 1988.

Manushi, nos. 50-52, *Devotional Women of India*. January-June 1989.

Nilsson, Usha S. *Mira Bai*. New Delhi: Sahitya Akademi, 1969.

Andrew Schelling

Andrew Schelling was born 14 January 1953 at St. Elizabeth's Hospital, Washington D.C. He spent the 1970s and '80s in Northern California where he studied ecology of mind with Gregory Bateson and poetry with Norman O. Brown. He also took up Sanskrit language and developed wilderness skills in the Sierra Nevada and Coast Range mountains. In 1990, he moved to Colorado to take work at Naropa University, where he teaches poetry and Sanskrit. Among his twenty-odd titles are *From the Arapaho Songbook* and *The Facts at Dog Tank Spring*. Another book, *Tracks Along the Left Coast: Jaime de Angulo & Pacific Coast Culture*, is a folkloric account of linguistics, old-time stories, poets, and cattle rustling in California. Besides *Songs of Mirabai*, he has seven books of translation from India's old languages, most recently *Songs of the Sons & Daughters of Buddha*, with Anne Waldman. Schelling lives in the "middle mountains," between the high plains and Colorado's Indian Peaks.

Arundhathi Subramaniam

Arundhathi Subramaniam is a poet, essay writer, and explorer of contemporary spiritual traditions in India. She has published a dozen books including *When God is a Traveller*, which received the Sahitya Akademi Award in 2020, and *Women Who Wear Only Themselves: Conversations with Four Travellers on Sacred Journeys*. Most recently she has edited *Wild Women, Seekers, Protagonists and Goddesses in Sacred Indian Poetry*, an anthology from Penguin. She lives in Mumbai.

Companions for the Journey Series

Inspirational work by well-known writers in a small-book format
designed to be carried along on your journey through life.

Volume 32
Songs of Mirabai
Translated by Andrew Schelling
978-1-945680-78-6.   137 pages

Volume 31
Homage to Green Tea
Ch'oŭi
Translated by Ian Haight & T'ae-yŏng Hŏ
978-1-945680-71-7.   109 pages

Volume 30
Returning Home: The Poetry of Tao Yuan-ming
Translated by Dan Veach
978-1-945680-69-4.   118 pages

Volume 29
Taken to Heart: 70 Poems from the Chinese
Translated by Gary Young and Yanwen Xu
978-1-945680-58-8.   104 pages

Volume 28
Dreaming of Fallen Blossoms
Tune Poems of Su Dong-Po
Translated by Yun Wang
978-1-945680-27-4   243 pages